Contents

Introduction

Welcome to Betty Bee's Handmade Wedding Crafts, where you will find a selection of projects to bring some crafty style to your big day. Whether you are a confident crafter or have never made anything before, all the projects featured are easy to achieve and have been written with busy lives in mind.

When I was asked to write this book, I admit I was thrilled. I'm what my friends refer to as a "wedding botherer"—I absolutely love them! I've photographed hundreds professionally and am regularly blown away at the thought, creativity, and attention to detail that goes into many people's big day. They are a tiny slice of theater and despite what many will tell you, they don't all have to be the same. The real joy of hand-making items for your big day is that they can be personal to you, so while you may want to follow some of the ideas featured in this book to the letter, others may simply be a great stepping-off point for your own creativity.

Remember, it's your wedding—
you are unique so why shouldn't your wedding be unique, too?

Handmade
Wedding Crafts

Handmade Wedding Crafts

35 vintage-inspired wedding projects for your special day

Betty Bee

CICO BOOKS

LONDON NEW YORK

*For Nick and the real Betty,
who rock my world, and in memory
of my dad, Sean.*

Published in 2012 by CICO Books
An imprint of Ryland Peters & Small Ltd
20–21 Jockey's Fields,
London WC1R 4BW
519 Broadway, 5th Floor,
New York, NY 10012

www.cicobooks.com

10 9 8 7 6 5 4 3 2 1

A CIP catalog record for this book is available from the Library
of Congress and the British Library.

ISBN: 978-1-908170-90-3

Printed in China

Editor: Katie Hardwicke
Designer: Mark Latter bluedragonfly-uk.com
Step-by-step photography: Nick Beedles
Style photography: Verity Welstead
Styling and art direction: Luis Peral-Aranda
Template illustrations: Stephen Dew

Craft-box essentials

Each project offers a comprehensive list of what you need, but the following items crop up again and again, so are worth investing in before you start.

Sewing machine
Needles and thread
Dressmaking shears and scissors—keep
   fabric scissors separate from paper
   scissors
Pinking shears
Unpicker (seam ripper)
Tape measure
Paper scissors, including decorative-edged
   craft scissors
PVA glue
Hot-glue gun with a good supply of glue
   sticks
Ribbons
Sequins and crystals
Buttons—look for vintage button boxes
   in thrift stores
Felt
Oddments of fabric
Pencil
Felt-tip pens or metallic pens
Ruler
Paper and card

Other useful equipment
Tools—basic home improvement tools, such
   as a drill, hammer, and pliers
Tool box—with screws, washers, wire, etc.
Safety goggles, dust mask, rubber gloves—
   to protect yourself on certain projects

Vintage finds

Several projects use items such as vintage lampshades, jewelry, tableware, buttons, and beads that can be sourced from thrift stores, flea markets, or auctions. Think of it as upcycling and a great way of using "something old" in your wedding plans. The quirky and nostalgic nature of preloved pieces will give an instant touch of shabby chic and vintage glamour to your projects.

Specialty craft materials

Some projects call for specific materials, like floral oasis balls and posy holders, or fascinators and hair combs, and these can all be easily sourced online or at craft stores. I have included a list of suppliers (see page 125) to help you locate everything you need to make your projects, and wedding preparations, run smoothly.

Marvelous mood boards

Once you start planning your wedding, it's a good idea to create mood boards—you can stick inspirational items in a large notebook to carry with you, or use a large sheet of card that you can add to when you discover something new. These are a great way to hone your vision of how you want your day to look, and often just one single item, such as an antique brooch or a faded photograph, can inform every element of your planning. When I create mood boards, I tear out images from magazines, scraps of fabric, jewelry, and even quotes and poetry. Use your mood board to record colors, fabrics, themes, and styles that sum up your individual vision. Whenever you feel you are losing focus, simply refer to your mood board and you will be back on track.

Chapter 1

Shabby Chic

Shabby-chic styling is the perfect way to use a traditional
wedding palette while introducing a touch of informal
elegance. A delicious combination of understated romance
and old-style charm, it works beautifully whatever the size
or style of your venue. For inspiration, think lavender
macaroons and petal perfect peonies. Displayed against
a backdrop of creamy, milk-colored linen and sparkling
glassware, this theme is wedding heaven sitting in a lightly
distressed chair.

Birdcage card holder

Guests will often bring greetings cards to weddings and having a dedicated place to collect them will ensure none get lost. I really love the look of old birdcages—they evoke such elegance and with a little dressing can look simply stunning.

you will need

Templates on page 118

Compass

Paper and pencil

Scissors

1 yd (1 m) white polyester fabric

Rubber or latex gloves

Pink and green fabric paint

Small paintbrushes

Tea light and lighter or matches

Bowl of water

Needle and thread

Buttons

Bright pink felt

Green wire

Hot-glue gun

Metal birdcage

Bird ornaments

Strands of (imitation) pearl beads

Tissue paper and feathers (optional)

1. Using the compass, draw and cut out three paper circles varying in size from small to large, using the templates on page 118. Use your circles as templates to cut out polyester petals. You will need six circles of each size per flower. I made six flowers.

2. Wearing gloves, paint a pink circle in the middle of each fabric circle. While the paint is still wet, use your fingers to rub the paint throughout the material. The effect isn't supposed to look neat, so don't panic if it looks a bit messy at this stage. Let dry thoroughly.

3. Light the tea light. Ensure you have a bowl of water next to you, in case your fabric catches light and you need to drop it into the water! Hold the fabric circle just above the tea light flame (don't let it touch it) and keep moving it round. The heat from the flame will gently bend the fabric so the edges start to curl inward and resemble petals. Do this with all your petal circles.

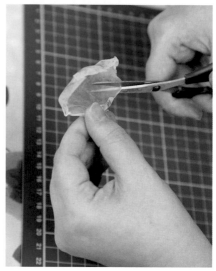

4. Use scissors to cut short slits toward the middle of each circle, but don't cut all the way to the center. Cut at regular intervals all the way round to create the individual petals.

5. Make up each flower by putting the biggest petals at the bottom and layering the smaller circles on top. Sew the layers together and finish off with a button to act as the flower's center.

6. Cut a small strip of felt about 2¼ in (6 cm) long and use a length of green wire to tie it in the middle, so it looks like a bow. Ensure there is enough wire left on either side to attach the flowers to the birdcage. Glue the felt to the back of your flower.

7. Using the same technique as with the flowers, cut about 15 leaf shapes out of the polyester and paint them green. Once dry, curl the edges with the tea light and then thread the leaves onto a 12-in (30-cm) long strand of green wire to form ivy. Make up about 8 strands of ivy.

8. Use your flowers, ivy, birds, and pearls to decorate your birdcage. Pink tissue paper and feathers inside the cage will add even more luxury. I printed out a little sign to put on the front of the cage so guests knew to use it as a very glamorous looking mailbox.

Betty's Top Tip

These also make gorgeous table centers instead of a more traditional floral display. If your wedding tables are themed, you can attach each table name to the cage and even place candies or favors inside.

Parasol with vintage lace

Parasols are a lovely way to keep the sun off a bride's face while she has her photographs taken. They are also a chic way to finish off your flower girls' outfits, especially if you match the colors to elements of their dresses.

you will need

Standard umbrella—choose one that is close to the color you want (for example, white or pink), so that the handle matches

Unpicker (seam ripper)

3¼ yd (3 m) lace

Scissors

Sewing machine

Needle and thread

Hot-glue gun

20 in (50 cm) chiffon

1. Carefully unpick the fabric from the umbrella. You will be left with the stripped-down frame and the nylon sections of the original umbrella's covering. Set the screw-in button from the top of the umbrella to one side, as you will need this later.

2. The umbrella's original covering is actually formed of six identical triangles of material. Use one of these as a pattern to cut out six pieces of your lace. Sew the six pieces of lace together. Leave a gap at the top approximately 1½ in (4 cm) wide. When finished, you will have what looks like a small lace underskirt.

3. Place the lace covering over the umbrella, using the hole at the top. Hand sew it into place on the underside, attaching the fabric to the umbrella spokes—use the holes in the metal frame from where the original covering was attached.

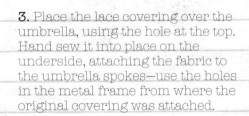

4. Screw the button from the top of the umbrella back in place. This will secure the fabric to the top. You can also spot glue your seams on the underside using a hot-glue gun.

5. Next, make the chiffon flowers to decorate your umbrella. Cut seven strips of chiffon approximately 20 x 2 in (50 x 5 cm). Fold over one end twice and stitch it to secure. Sew a running stitch all the way along the strip of fabric, folding the fabric in and out as you go to create a concertina effect.

6. Once you get to the end, pull the thread tight to gather the strip into a flower and secure the gathers with a few small stitches. Sew the flowers on the top of your umbrella and on each section for added prettiness.

Betty's Top Tip

To ensure rain doesn't spoil your wedding, invest in some black and white umbrellas and tie parcel tags to the handles inviting people to use them. If you do encounter a few showers, particularly during the outdoor photographs, these will save the day and many a hairdo!

"Tie the knot" save-the-date cards

Once you have decided on your wedding date, it's important to ensure all your guests mark it in their calendar. Save-the-date cards mean you can tell people when you are getting married before you have finalized any other arrangements. These save-the-date cards are a great play on words. "Tying the knot" has long been a saying associated with getting married and years ago people would tie a knot in their handkerchiefs to remember things by.

you will need

Square blank card in a color to match your theme

Scalpel or craft knife, metal rule, and cutting mat

Scissors

Sequins and beads

A length of fabric—you can use an actual handkerchief if you prefer, but I used white organza

Needle and thread

Hot-glue gun

Paper glue

Metallic pen

1. Open out your blank card and using a scalpel and cutting mat, cut two slits into the center of the front cover approximately 1¼ in (3 cm) long and 1¼ in (3 cm) apart. Use scissors to cut the right-hand corner of the card away to make a scalloped edge.

2. Decorate the front of your card with sequins, feathers, or any other embellishments that tie into your wedding theme.

3. Use the hot-glue gun to attach decoration to the edges of your handkerchief or fabric. I used pink sequins. Let the glue dry.

4. Once your handkerchief is dry, thread it through the two slits on the front of the card and tie a knot. You can stitch this in place to further secure it and add a little more embellishment for a final touch, if you like.

5. Write the date of your wedding on the exposed top corner on the inside of the card with a metallic pen, not forgetting to add your names inside.

Betty's Top Tip

If you already know who you would like to act as your bridesmaids and best man, you can personalize the save the date card further and include this request as well. These guys are vital to the smooth running of your wedding day, so ensuring they feel special from the very beginning is no bad thing.

"Something Old" lace bridal shoes

Your wedding shoes are possibly the most important footwear you will ever own. Embellishing a simple pair of white high-heeled shoes not only means that they are unique but also, with a little forward planning, that you can incorporate "something old" with a little vintage lace. If you are very lucky, you may be able to use a small piece from your mother's wedding dress or your christening gown (ask first!) but if not, finding old lace handkerchiefs is quite easy at flea markets or thrift stores.

you will need

Pair of white wedding shoes

Vintage lace

Scissors

Crystal gems

Hot-glue gun

Tweezers

Ribbon

1. Measure a piece of lace to fit across the toe of your shoe. This is the part that will be seen the most as it peaks out from under your dress, so deserves special attention. Carefully add glue to the edges of your shoe and fix the lace. You can tidy the edge of the lace with a scalpel or sharp scissors once it is dry.

2. Fix crystals onto the edge of the lace with the glue gun, applying the glue to the back of the crystal rather than the lace for a neater finish. If you are using particularly small crystals, use a pair of tweezers to help you position them.

3. Tie a small bow with a length of ribbon and glue this at the top of each lace toe panel. You could use blue ribbon to add "something blue" to your outfit.

4. Apply two small panels of lace to the back of each shoe and then add crystals along the seam. You can also add crystals along the top edge of the shoe.

5. The finishing touch is to glue a crystal heart or flower on the bottom of your shoes. This is a particularly nice idea if you will be kneeling as part of the wedding service—the congregation will see the sparkle as you kneel before the priest or vicar. You can even write "I do" in crystals, or your new initials.

6. Enjoy your fabulously glamorous wedding shoes!

Betty's Top Tip

Remember, it's always a good idea to wear in new shoes to avoid blisters. Wear your wedding shoes around the house with socks for a few days in advance of the ceremony, so that you glide rather than hobble down the aisle.

Ribbon-rose posy

There can be few more satisfying wedding crafts than ribbon roses. After a little practice it takes a matter of minutes to make them and they have so many uses— add them to corsages and dresses, or make beautiful table centers. These posies are particularly lovely for flower girls and bridesmaids as they are very light to carry.

you will need

Approx 3¼ yd (3 m) satin ribbon for roses—the width of the ribbon will determine the size of your roses; I used 1¼-in (3-cm) wide ribbon

Hot-glue gun

Plastic flower stems or covered pipe cleaners

Extra ribbon for bow

1. Cut a length of ribbon approximately 8 in (20 cm) long. Tie a knot approximately 1½ in (4 cm) from the end of your ribbon, leaving a short "tail" hanging down.

2. Holding onto the knot, fold the long length of ribbon inward and round above the knot three times. This will create your inner rose bud. Secure the bud with a dot of hot glue.

3. Keeping hold of the bottom of your inner rose bud, bring the ribbon up on a diagonal (fold it up and across) and wrap it around the bud once. Repeat this action to create folds of ribbon that resemble petals. Use a dot of hot glue every time you wrap the ribbon around to secure it. How tightly you wrap the ribbon will affect the size and shape of your rose. As you make a few, you can decide on your preferred shape.

4. Once you have reached the end of the ribbon, glue it neatly underneath the rose.

5. Take a pair of small scissors and gently poke the inside of your flower so it all sits tightly.

6. Take your plastic stem or pipe cleaner and dot hot glue on the end. Gently push this through the bottom of your rose until it is about halfway inside.

Betty's Top Tip

You can use this technique to create matching buttonholes for your groom and ushers. Simply cut the stem quite short and use the ribbon tail to cover it completely. This gives you something to anchor the pin into from the back of the lapel.

7. Wrap the ribbon tail around the top of the stem and stick it down with hot glue. Repeat these steps until you have at least fifteen roses. Tie them together using a length of ribbon, finished with a bow. Your ribbon posy is complete.

Birdcage veil

A small birdcage veil looks incredibly chic and is a great alternative to wearing flowers or a longer veil in your hair. The shape and materials used in this fascinator would complement most wedding-dress styles and can, of course, be adapted to suit your theme.

you will need

Hot-glue gun

White feathers—I used marabou as I wanted the fascinator to be fluffy like a bird's tail, but you can go for a sleeker option

White teardrop sinamay base

Pencil or craft tool

White netting

White doves decoration

Plastic hair comb

Scissors

Felt

Ribbon

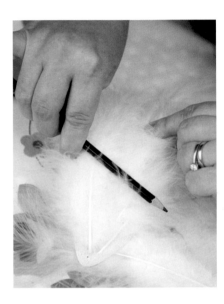

1. Put a drop of glue on the tip of each feather and attach them in rows to your sinamay base. The desired effect is to look like a bird's plumage, so keep this in mind as you create your shape. Use a pencil to gently press each feather for a second or two to ensure it is stuck down properly.

2. Cut out your veil shape. I used approximately 8 in (20 cm) square. If your material has a scalloped edge or pattern, keep this in mind when attaching it. To create the birdcage effect, pull the two side edges of the veil under slightly and use a tiny spot of glue to secure. Press with the pencil to ensure the edges are joined. This should create a good curved shape.

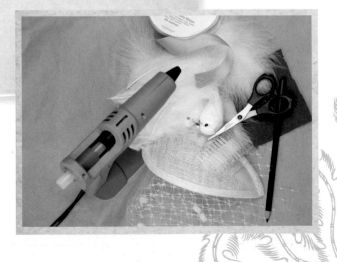

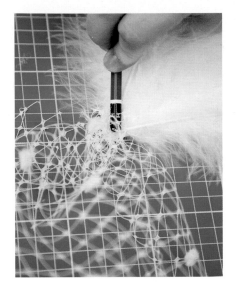

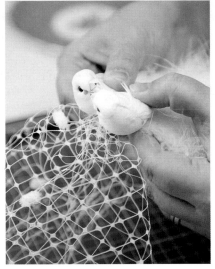

3. Gather the top of the veil fabric together and glue it to the narrowest part of your base. You may want to see how the veil sits best on the base using pins to ensure you get the right position.

4. Now glue your bird decoration onto the base to cover where the veil is attached.

5. Measure the length of your hair comb and cut out a thin strip of felt to match. Glue this to the underside of your base at the point where you want it to attach to your head (keep in mind how you will be wearing your hair on the day).

6. Glue a length of ribbon to the top of your hair comb, covering the front and back. Attach it to the sinamay base on the strip of felt (this will ensure it is quite secure). Let the glue dry fully before wearing it—bridal hair and hot glue is never a good mix!

Betty's Top Tip

You can use small round sinamays to create mini versions of this veil for your bridesmaids. Match the color of the birds and netting to their outfits or flowers.

Bringing a sense of the outdoors to your wedding works particularly well at spring receptions and nothing says garden better than a classic plant pot. Using wooden flowers adds another clever twist and, most importantly of all, it looks gorgeous!

you will need

Terra-cotta plant pot

White spray paint

Dust mask

Sandpaper

Tissue paper

Wooden flowers

Pliers

Oasis floral foam ball (to fit the diameter of the pot)

Ribbon

1. Spray your terra-cotta pot with white spray paint either outdoors or in a well-ventilated room wearing a dust mask. Let it dry completely, then go over it lightly with sandpaper to create a worn look. Stuff your pot with tissue paper.

2. Use pliers to cut the stems of your wooden flowers so they are approximately 2 in (5 cm) long.

Betty's Top Tip

You can also make entire balls of flowers and hang them at your wedding reception on ribbons.

3. Gently poke the flowers into the oasis ball. If you are using more than one color, make sure that you space them evenly. You need only fill the top half of the oasis ball with the flowers.

4. Press the oasis ball into the pot and tie a ribbon around the rim—your table center is complete!

Ring pillow

Avoid any worries about wedding bands being dropped during the service by making this pretty ring pillow. Its ribbons will secure the rings, ready to be slipped on the bride and groom's fingers as they exchange vows.

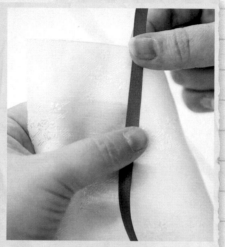

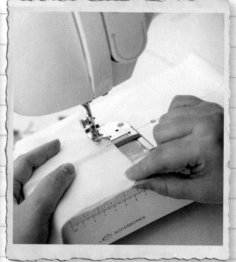

you will need

Fabric, cut into two pieces, each 5 x 6 in (12.5 x 15 cm)

Two lengths of ribbon, each 15 in (38 cm)

Sewing machine

Fiberfill (polyester) stuffing

Needle and thread

Ribbon buckles

Feather

Hot-glue gun

Ribbon rose

1. Place one piece of fabric with the right side up. Measure and mark the center on each of the short sides with a pencil. Pin a length of ribbon to each of these marks, with approximately 1 in (2.5 cm) extending beyond the edge.

2. Place the second piece of fabric on top, so that right sides are together, with the ribbon on the inside. Sew the fabric together on the sewing machine (catching the ribbon on the edges), with a ¼ in (5 mm) seam allowance, leaving a gap of about 2 in (5 cm) in one long side for turning through. Take care not to sew the long ends of the ribbon into the seams.

Betty's Top Tip

When tying your rings to the pillow a simple bow will suffice. Avoid knots or you could hold up the service while the best man attempts to get them free!

3. Turn the pillow the right way out through the gap. Push the corners out to make a neat finish and then fill the pillow with small amounts of stuffing until it is firm. Hand sew the gap neatly with slip stitches.

4. Thread an equal number of ribbon buckles onto each of your attached ribbon pieces until you get to the middle. Dab a spot of hot glue on the center of the pillow and add a white feather, then glue a ribbon rose on top of this so it sits just above where your ribbon bow will be. Your rings are now ready to be tied on and secured with a bow.

Cupcake candles

These cupcake-shaped candles make beautiful wedding favors. You can even place them in individual cake boxes for each guest. Of course, they also look cute as a button placed around your wedding cake—don't forget they aren't edible though!

you will need

10 oz (300 g) soy wax pellets

Glass or heatproof pitcher (jug) or measuring cup

Scented oil

Wooden skewers and elastic bands

Silicon cupcake molds

Tea-light wicks and wick sustainers

Wooden or plastic fork (the kind you get with takeouts)

Candle glitter

Paper cupcake cases

1. To make a batch of five cupcake candles, fill the pitcher (jug) to the top with wax pellets and heat in a microwave on high for approximately two minutes, or until it reaches melting point and is clear. Add a few drops of scented oil and stir them in with a wooden skewer.

2. Attach a sustainer to the end of the wick and place it in the center of your silicon mold. Pour in the wax so that it reaches the top of the mold.

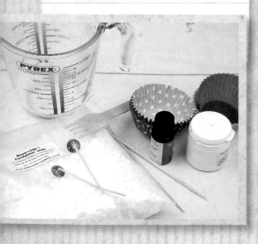

Betty's Top Tip

Candy-colored china teacup saucers make great holders for these candles. Alternatively, you can fill a cake stand with them and light them for your evening reception.

3. Attach two skewers together at both ends with elastic bands, then thread the wick between them and rest the skewers on the mold. This keeps the wick straight as the wax sets.

4. Just before the wax sets completely, take the fork and swirl the top of the wax so that it resembles frosting. Sprinkle on some glitter and snip your wick to the desired length. Take the candles out of their molds and put them into paper cases, but always remember to remove them from these before you light them.

Butterfly bouquet

Butterflies, with their delicate wings and beautiful colors, are a lovely theme for a wedding, particularly one in the spring or summer. This bouquet is made to look as if the bride is holding a posy full of butterflies ready to fly away. It's very light, so perfect if you don't want to hold something heavy all day. You can extend the theme to your table centers, too, by following the same steps and placing the butterfly posies in simple glass vases.

you will need

Feather butterflies, about 20

Jewelry wire

Small pair of scissors

Hot-glue gun

Pipe cleaners

20 in (50 cm) ribbon

Decorative pins

1. Use the point of the scissors to make a small hole in the back of each butterfly. Cut a 16-in (40-cm) length of jewelry wire for each butterfly. Dab a few drops of hot glue into the hole you have created.

2. Put one end of the wire into the hole in the back of the butterfly and press it down, using the end of a pencil or craft tool (not your fingers—the glue is hot!) to ensure it is really secure.

3. Once you have about twenty butterflies, gather them together and tie the stem tightly with some more jewelry wire.

4. Now wrap some pipe cleaners around the metal wire stem. This will fill the stem out making it look more substantial and it will also be more comfortable to hold.

5. Wrap ribbon tightly from the bottom of the stem up to the top—dab hot glue at the start and end, and at regular intervals on the underside of the ribbon to secure it in place. Push a few decorative pins in along the stem.

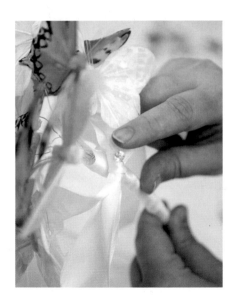

6. Tie a bow at the top of the posy with a length of ribbon and secure it with a decorative pin. Glue a single butterfly underneath the bow to finish the posy.

Betty's Top Tip

A lovely variation on this theme would be birds and butterflies—simply dot as many bird decorations as you like throughout the bouquet in contrasting colors.

Chapter 2

Quirky Glamour

If you are someone who loves to explore different design ideas, a wedding is the perfect opportunity to let your individuality shine through. Quirky glamour is all about subverting traditional ideas—think of it like arts and crafts with a sprinkle of fairy dust—with bold colors, unusual materials, and lots of ingenuity. Tweeds replace chiffon, buttons might be used instead of flowers, and where possible elements of creative "upcycling" shine through. It's witty and stylish—and there are no rules.

Pinwheel bouquet and buttonholes

Incorporate a little seaside Victoriana into your wedding with these delightful pinwheels, or "whirligigs" as our grandparents would have called them. These pinwheels can be created in a matter of hours and used either as an alternative to a bouquet or as a prop for your wedding photographs. Small versions can also be made and worn as buttonholes and corsages.

you will need

Template on page 123

Patterned paper or card

Pencil and ruler

Scissors

Hole punch

Paper fasteners

PVA glue

Garden canes (or lollipop sticks for the buttonholes)

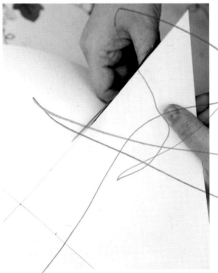

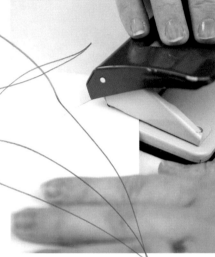

1. Copy the template on page 123 onto a piece of card or patterned paper. Cut along each marked line, stopping where indicated, about 1½ in (4 cm) from the center. Use the sharp end of your scissors to make a hole in the center.

2. Position your hole punch over the marked dot on the left side at the top of each corner, and make a single hole with the hole punch.

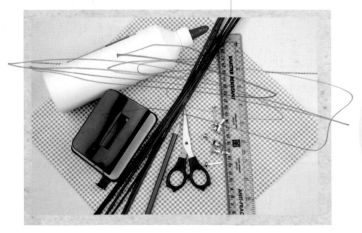

Betty's Top Tip

Photo paper is the perfect material for making pinwheels. If you have a photo printer at home, have some fun and print out special snaps, such as memories of holidays or baby photos. Anything that sums up the happy couple can be used to make the pinwheels.

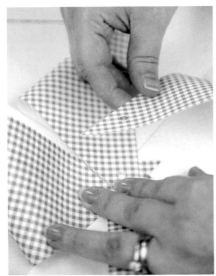

3. Bring each outer corner with a hole into the center, holding them down with your finger and lining up the holes. You should see the pinwheel shape emerge. Insert a paper fastener through the holes and spread the fasteners on the back.

4. Dab glue on the top of your garden cane or lollipop stick, and stick to the back of the pinwheel and then secure the fastener around the stick. Repeat to make as many pinwheels as required.

Button bouquet

One of the most exciting things I found at a recent auction was a tin of old buttons. If you are an enthusiastic dressmaker, incorporating buttons and bows into your wedding design is a lovely nod to your hobbies and for the ultimate in stylish upcycling it is hard to beat. This bouquet can incorporate your something old, new, borrowed, and blue with just a few simple button selections. Be careful not to throw this though, as it is quite heavy!

you will need

Template on page 119

Pencil and card

Felt in assorted colors

Scissors

Needle and colored embroidery floss (thread)

Assorted buttons

Jewelry wire

Colored thread

20 in (50 cm) ribbon, plus extra for bow (optional)

Decorative pins

Hot-glue gun

1. Trace the template on page 119 and make a flower template from card. Use this to cut out flowers from the felt. The thicker the felt the more structure your bouquet will have, so either choose a thick felt or double up your layers. Sew the edges using a blanket stitch in a contrasting color embroidery floss.

2. Cut a length of jewelry wire approximately 16 in (40 cm) long. Thread each end of the wire through the holes in your buttons—either use a single large button or layer a few in differing sizes and colors to create a more 3-D shape. Once your button is threaded through, twist the wire tightly underneath to form a stem.

3. Poke the wire stem through the center of the felt flower. The wire should be sharp enough to go through unaided, but you can always use an unpicker or a needle to create a hole first. Pull your button stem through and then twist it underneath so the felt flower and buttons are firmly attached to each other.

4. Repeat these steps until you have at least fifteen stems. Arrange your button flowers into a posy and tie the stems together using jewelry wire.

5. . Cover the wire stem with ribbon, wrapping it tightly from the bottom to the top—dab hot glue at the start and end, and at regular intervals on the underside of the ribbon to secure it in place. Push a few decorative pins in along the stem to add some sparkle. You can tie a bow around the top with extra ribbon, if you like.

Flower boutonnières

To continue the button theme throughout your wedding, why not make button boutonnières (or buttonholes)?

1. Using jewelry wire, create a small button tree with three or four stems of layered buttons.

2. Wrap the ends together and sew the stem onto a felt flower. Cover the stem with a length of ribbon. These can be attached to the groom's lapel with a decorative pin.

Medal-style boutonnières

You could also easily fashion a medal-style boutonnière.

Glue buttons onto a strip of ribbon and then attach it to an old brace holder. Hook the boutonnière over a button or attach it in place with a safety pin from the back of the lapel.

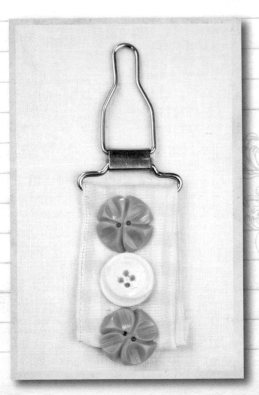

Button napkin holders

These look lovely tied around colored linen and are a simple way to introduce your key wedding colors into your reception table scheme.

Thread a few buttons onto a length of jewelry wire, using different sizes and colors. Turn each end over so they are not sharp. The lovely thing about buttons is the variety of looks you can create—for a folksy, muted palette, combine leather and bone-colored buttons or, if you want sparkle, use diamanté encrusted pieces.

Betty's Top Tip

Ask friends and family to donate buttons to your wedding project. You will be amazed at the lovely buttons you will be given and using those given by loved ones adds even more meaning to what you make. Big buttons, especially embellished ones, can be expensive, so scour flea markets and yard sales. Sometimes it's cheaper to buy old cardigans and jackets for the buttons than it is to buy them new from haberdashery stores, and there is also a sense of history from using pre-loved buttons, too.

Felt flower table center

Felt is a wonderful material to work with when crafting and gives a fantastic 3-D quality to your homemade creations. It is perfect if you want to incorporate a magical "Alice in Wonderland" aspect into your wedding. With just a few simple tricks you can transform squares of brightly colored felt into striking bouquets, table centerpieces, and buttonholes.

you will need

Template on page 119
Pipe cleaners
Green floral tape
Colored felt
Scissors
Pencil
Hot-glue gun
Small buttons
Glass jar

1. To make the flower stems, take a pipe cleaner and cut it to the length you require—test it in your jar or vase to ensure your flowers will be attractively displayed. Starting from one end, tightly wrap green tape around the pipe cleaner. I found by sticking the tape at the end I could twirl the pipe cleaner into the tape as I pulled it off the roll and this made for a neat finish.

2. To make the flower, cut a circle of felt using the template on page 119. Cut a spiral working inward, following the guide on the template. When you approach the center, leave a large circle almost like a comma—this will form the base of your flower.

3. Take a pencil and wrap the felt around it until you have used about half the length of felt. Remove the wound spiral from the pencil and continue rolling until you reach the center circle.

4. Dab a spot of hot glue on the center of the rolled shape, press your pre-prepared stem on the glue, and simply cover with the circle end of your spiral. This will form your flower shape.

5. Use a dab of hot glue to attach a button to the front of the felt flower, to make the flower center. Repeat these steps to make as many flowers as required to fill your vase.

6. Finally, glue a strip of felt around your glass jar or vase, overlapping the ends a little for a neat finish. Attach a simple button to tie the theme together.

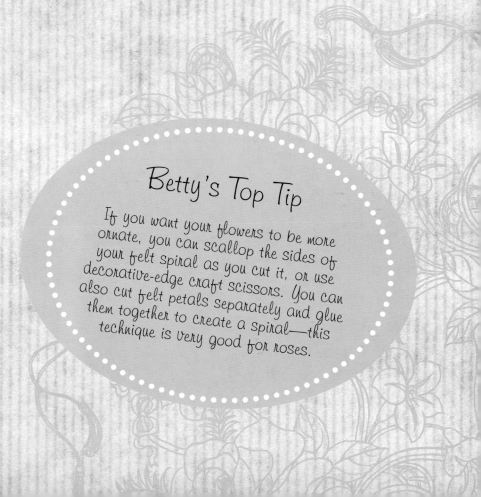

Betty's Top Tip

If you want your flowers to be more ornate, you can scallop the sides of your felt spiral as you cut it, or use decorative-edge craft scissors. You can also cut felt petals separately and glue them together to create a spiral—this technique is very good for roses.

Red, white, and blue flower crates

There is something quintessentially old-fashioned about milk bottles in crates, which is what inspired me to create this project. It is a humorous take on wedding flower displays—the arrangement will still look beautiful but with an informal, vintage feel.

you will need

Wooden crate

Paintbrush

White latex (emulsion) paint

Milk bottles

Red, white, and blue enamel
   spray paint

Dust mask

Protective gloves

Red, white, and blue striped
   ribbon

PVA glue

Printed postcard or sign with
   the bride's and groom's
   names on it

1. Paint your wooden crate inside and out with white paint. For a distressed look, use just one coat with a large brush.

2. Spray your milk bottles with spray paint either outdoors or in a well-ventilated space wearing the dust mask and gloves. The bottles will need two coats and should look almost like they are made of china or porcelain when they are dry.

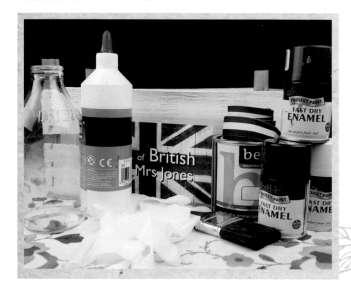

Betty's Top Tip

Glass bottles and jars holding just a single flower or candle are a great way to break from modern uniformity and a clever way to keep fresh flower costs down. Decorate bottles with string, ribbon, or glass paint and use just one striking container or a small group of glassware. These will catch the light wonderfully.

3. Cut a length of ribbon, wrap it around the neck of the bottle, and fold it. Glue the ends over to resemble a bow.

4. Glue your sign to the front of your crate and put single flower stems in each bottle. To stop the bottles moving, you may want to pad your crate with some tissue paper or sisal.

A key part of any wedding is the photography. Not all guests enjoy having their photo taken so a good way to break the ice and get people to relax is to give them silly props for a few shots. These lips and mustaches are great fun and very simple to make.

you will need

Templates on page 121

Thick cardboard

Pencil

Scissors

Red and black spray paint

Dust mask

Red glitter

Wooden coffee stirrers

Superglue

1. Copy the templates on page 121 and transfer them onto cardboard. Cut out the lips and moustache shapes, making enough for a group photo or to match the table plan.

2. Protect your work surface with a large sheet of newspaper or scrap paper, and spray your shape—red for lips and black for moustaches. Work in a well-ventilated space and wear a dust mask. While the lip shapes are still wet, sprinkle with glitter.

3. Dab a spot of glue onto the end of a coffee stirrer. Stick it to the side of your shape on the back, not the center.

4. Fill up jars with your photo props and dot them around your reception. You can also make spectacles, speech bubbles, and even hearts—anything that will add some silliness to your photos.

Cocktail-glass cake stand

If vintage china isn't your thing but you would still love to use cake stands as table centers, then this idea is perfect. You can make these as tiered stands but they look particularly glamorous as single tiers, and the colors can be chosen to tie in perfectly with your scheme.

you will need

Standard ceramic plate

Cocktail or large wine glass

Spray paint—ensure it can be used on glass and ceramics

Glass glue

Dust mask

Note

As with anything that has been sprayed with paint, ensure any food or cakes are in cases and not in direct contact with the plate.

1. Ensure your plate and glass are dry, clean, and dust-free. Protect your work surface with newspaper and work outdoors or in a well-ventilated space. Wearing a dust mask, spray all surfaces of your glass and plate with two coats of colored paint— wait for the first coat to dry completely before applying the second. If you spray from a slight distance you will avoid any drips and achieve an even finish.

2. Once your plate and glass are fully painted and dry, apply a thin coat of glass glue to the rim of the glass.

3. Turn the plate over and attach the glass to the center. Turn the stand upright and weight the plate with something heavy, like a book. Let dry for about 12 hours. Your stand will be strong enough to hold cakes, fruit, or flowers.

Outdoor standard lamp

Standard lamps add an instant dash of old-fashioned style to any event and with this approach you can use them outside as well as indoors. If you are having a garden party reception or using a marquee, these lamps can safely add light without any power supply.

you will need

Old standard lamp and shade—it doesn't need to be in working order

Tape measure

Scissors

Fabric—this project is particularly eye-catching if you use two contrasting fabrics

Pins

Hot-glue gun

Trimmings to decorate the shade

White spray paint or latex (emulsion) paint and paintbrush

Dust mask

Protective gloves

Sandpaper

Ribbon (optional)

Battery-operated bulb

1. Remove the lampshade. Measure the length and width of the lampshade panels. Cut fabric panels to the same measurements, allowing a little extra for turning under edges, and pin these over the existing lampshade fabric so you can check you are happy that they fit correctly.

2. Attach each fabric panel with the hot glue gun, turning under the raw edges to give a neat finish and running the glue along each seam.

3. Glue trimmings at the top of the shade and along the bottom to create fringing. This will not only make your lamp look classically vintage, but also neaten up the appearance of the fabric panels by tying it all together.

4. Remove the light fitting from the top of the lamp base. Working in a well-ventilated space or outdoors and wearing a dust mask and gloves, spray the lamp base with white paint, or alternatively paint with normal paint.

5. Once the paint is dry, lightly sand the lamp base in patches to give it a classic shabby-chic look. You can also tie ribbons down the base for added prettiness.

6. Use hot glue to fix the battery-operated light bulb to the top of the lamp base, then fix the shade onto the stand. Your outdoor standard lamp is now ready to light up your wedding reception.

Betty's Top Tip

Create mini lounge areas at your reception: a few comfortable chairs, a standard lamp, and some footstools will create lovely little homely pockets for guests to relax in.

Bow-tie corsage

These bow-tie style corsages make a unique alternative to traditional flowers. Use pretty fabrics so they look like a bow, or opt for tweeds and cord for an altogether more masculine look.

you will need

Piece of fabric, 3 x 20 in (8 x 50 cm) for the main bow

Piece of fabric, 3 x 4 in (8 x 10 cm) for the middle of the bow

Sewing machine

Needle and thread

Piece of ribbon or bias binding to wear around the wrist

Sticky-back Velcro

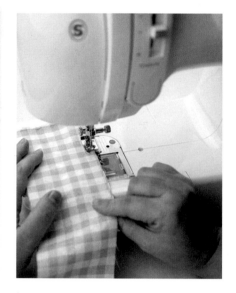

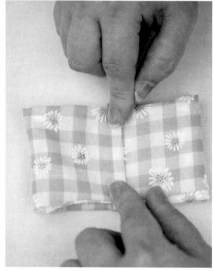

1. Fold your main piece of fabric in half lengthwise, with right sides facing, and sew one short side and the long side together on a sewing machine to create a long thin tube, leaving one end open.

2. Turn the tube right side out through the end. Fold each end in to the middle, overlapping slightly. Sew down the middle to secure the ends together. This will form the main part of your bow.

3. Repeat step 1 with the smaller piece of fabric to make the middle "tie" of the bow, turning it right sides out.

Betty's Top Tip

These little bow ties also work as hair fascinators for bridesmaids and you could make them for all your ushers to wear instead of the usual tie.

4. Pinch your main bow together in the middle and sew a few stitches through it to hold the gathers. Wrap your middle piece around the center of the bow and sew it neatly at the back. This finishes off your bow tie.

5. Measure your wrist and add a little extra for seams, then cut a piece of ribbon to this length. Machine sew a small hem at each end of the ribbon to prevent it fraying. Cut two pieces of Velcro and sew one piece on the inside end and one on the outside end to make a seamless join when fastened together.

6. Hand sew your bow tie onto the middle of the wrist ribbon band and your corsage is ready.

Bride-and-groom brandy glasses

Regardless of the style of wedding you choose, there is little doubt that a few toasts will be made to the new bride and groom. For very little cost you can create personalized glasses that will not only look suitably fetching on your wedding table but which you can also keep afterward as a memento.

you will need

Templates on page 121

Two glasses—you can find these in thrift stores or yard sales

Glass paint pens

Glass adhesive

Crystal gems

1. Choose your design—I chose a pink lipsticked mouth to denote the bride and a mustache for the groom. You may want to try out a few ideas on a spare glass first—you could add "Mr" and "Mrs" and your wedding date as well.

2. Ensure your glass is clean and dry. Start to decorate the glasses using the glass paint pens, adding a pretty pattern around the rim.

3. Ensuring that you leave space for the main design, decorate the glass further with small crystal gems. Dab a small amount of glue on the back of each crystal and attach to the glass. These look particularly good around the bottom of the stem and dotted around the main part of the glass.

4. Draw on your main design either freehand or copy the templates on page 121. Draw the outline first, let it dry and then fill in solid areas between the outlines. Allow to dry thoroughly before using.

Betty's Top Tip

I've used brandy glasses as their bell shape lends itself to painting on but you can use any style you like, from champagne flutes to beer glasses. Wash the decorated glasses by hand only.

Chapter 3

Fabulous Vintage

Looking to the past for style influences has long been
a trick used by fashion designers and artists as a matter
of course. Certain eras lend themselves beautifully
to wedding styling, and for me nothing beats the 1940s
and 50s. It has an optimistic, homespun flavor that is
just made for weddings.

China-teacup table centerpiece

Make a beautiful table display using vintage china. The cups don't have to match—in fact, it can look prettier if they don't. However, I try to tie them together with a theme (birds, flowers, or toile, for example) or with complementary colors.

you will need

Three-tier cake stand fixing

White enamel paint

Small paintbrush

Three teacups and one saucer

Tape measure

Pen

Fully charged cordless drill with a tile drill bit—this is important, as a normal drill bit will break the china

Safety goggles

Screws and washers

Screwdriver

Flowers

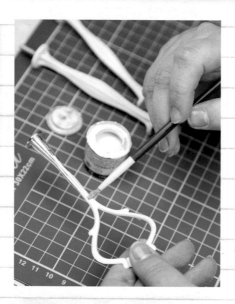

1. Paint the cake stand fixing with white paint. You can leave this gold but the white makes it look more like a whole unit with the china.

2. Make sure the saucer and teacups are clean and dry. For each one, measure the diameter of the plate or cup and mark the center with a pen. This will act as your drill guide.

3. Time to put on the safety goggles! Find somewhere to drill the saucer and teacup where they won't slip and you won't drill into something precious underneath—a workbench is ideal.

4. Put a small amount of water in the saucer and the teacup to keep the drill bit and china cold. Slowly drill each piece through the center marking you made in step 2.

5. Assemble the cake stand, starting with the saucer. Put a washer on the base and then push the bottom screw into the plate. Put a washer on the topside of the plate and then fix the cake-stand fitting. Add a washer and attach the first cup, then continue until all three fixings and teacups have been attached.

6. Fill each cup with small budded flowers. The size of the cups means you can create beautiful floral displays without using huge amounts of flowers—thrifty as well as beautiful.

Betty's Top Tip

You can also use this method to make classic cake stands. Simply use a large dinner plate, a side plate, and a saucer to create the different-sized tiers.

Mini-jar wedding favors

The tradition of giving guests sugared almonds to signify well wishes from the bride and groom is centuries old. Rather than using the usual chiffon bags, channel your inner domestic goddess and use tiny glass jars instead.

you will need

Saucer or small plate

Pencil

Fabric

Pinking shears

Mini glass jars

Sugared almonds

Elastic bands

Ribbon

Self-adhesive labels

1. Position the plate on the fabric and draw around it to create a circle. Cut it out using pinking shears—these will give a lovely old-fashioned scalloped edge.

2. Fill the jar with sugared almonds and replace the lid. Position the fabric circle over the lid and secure it with an elastic band.

3. Cut a length of ribbon and tie it over the elastic band, finishing with a pretty bow.

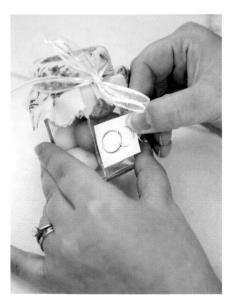

4. Attach a sticky label to the jar. This could be handwritten or printed, perhaps with the name of the bride and groom and the date, a photograph, or a special message to your guests thanking them for coming.

Betty's Top Tip

Fill your jars with homemade conserve rather than almonds to create a wedding favor that your guests can spread on their toast the following morning.

Fabric bunting

Bunting is such a simple yet effective way to evoke vintage nostalgia with your wedding decorations, quickly transforming a church hall or reception room into a festive place of loveliness— and it's so easy to make.

you will need

Template on page 120

Pencil

Card or cardboard—a cereal box works well

Tailor's chalk (optional)

Scissors

½ yd (½ m) fabric in total—if you'd like lots of different patterns (and this looks very pretty), look for ready-cut selections for patchwork or quilting

Sewing machine—or you could easily sew these by hand

4⅓ yd (4 m) white bias binding or fabric tape

Pins

1. Copy the template on page 120 and make a pattern from thick card or cardboard. Attach the template to the fabric, or draw round it with tailor's chalk, and cut out triangles. You will need 24 triangles to make 12 double-sided bunting flags.

2. Take two triangles (either matching or in different patterns) and place them right sides together. Sew them together all they way round, taking a ¼-in (5-mm) seam and leaving a 1¼-in (3-cm) gap in the top to turn them out. Repeat to make 12 bunting flags in total.

3. Snip the points off the corners of each triangle, being careful not to cut through the stitching. Turn the flags out through the gap in the top. You can use a pencil to poke out the corners to make them sharp.

4. Pin your bunting into the fold in the fabric tape, leaving a 1¼-in (3-cm) gap between each. Sew along the tape to attach the bunting. Give your bunting a quick press and it's ready to be hung.

Betty's Top Tip

Why not personalize your bunting by making it out of old T-shirts or college sweatshirts? Think of it as a patchwork quilt—perhaps family members could each donate a piece of fabric.

Keepsake vintage brooch bouquet

This is a beautiful alternative to real flowers—you can keep the brooch bouquet for ever and it is perfect for incorporating "something old, something new" into your wedding. Collecting the brooches from thrift stores or flea markets may take time, so this is a lovely project to start as soon as you have set your wedding date.

you will need

Plastic posy holder

Large oasis floral foam ball

Strong tape

½ yd (½ m) fabric to cover the oasis, such as a white silk mix

Garden wire—strong enough to hold the brooch but bendable

Scissors or pliers to cut wire

Brooches—for a large bouquet you will need about 40

Hot-glue gun

Craft knife or scalpel

Skewer or chopstick

Masking tape

Ribbon

Feathers

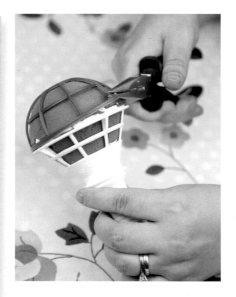

1. Remove the plastic cage and small ball of oasis from your posy holder. Tape the bigger oasis ball onto the handle using strong tape. Cut the end off your posy holder stem with a pair of scissors.

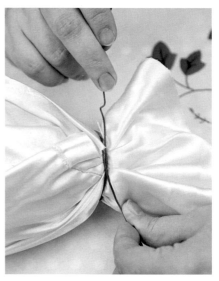

2. Cover the oasis ball with the silk fabric, smoothing it flat. Wrap a length of wire around the fabric at the top of the handle to secure and then trim the excess fabric.

3. For each brooch cut a length of wire the full length of the bouquet and then half again. Hot glue the brooch clasps shut. Twist the precut wire onto the back of the clasp and wind it around a few times so it is secure. Repeat this process for all the brooches.

4. Make a small hole through the fabric-covered oasis ball with a craft knife or scalpel, or a small pair of scissors.

5. Use masking tape to stick the end of the brooch wire to the end of a skewer. Poke the skewer through the ready-made hole and then push it all the way down the stem of the posy holder. When you can see the bottom of the skewer poking out, remove the masking tape and pull the wire through. Hold onto the end of the wire while you pull the skewer out.

6. Pull the wire up over the posy handle and wrap it around the neck of the bouquet to secure it. Repeat steps 4 to 6 until the whole oasis ball is covered in brooches. Tape the wires firmly to the stem so they are flush and neat.

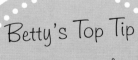

Betty's Top Tip

I glued the brooches to further secure them and stop the bouquet rattling, but if the odd brooch is of sentimental value you can leave out this step.

7. Glue a piece of ribbon to the end of the posy holder to cover it and then wrap ribbon up the stem, securing with glue as you go. Take the ribbon up the whole handle to cover all the wires.

8. Stick feathers in any little gaps between the brooches. I also spot-glued the brooches so the whole bouquet felt really secure. Finish with a contrasting bow.

Fork place-name holders

Old cutlery is surprisingly easy to pick up at auctions or flea markets and can be quickly turned into elegant-looking place-name holders. This is often a project the groom quite enjoys, as really all it requires is a little brute force!

you will need

Forks

Two sets of pliers

Place-name cards

1. Hold the handle of a fork in one pair of pliers just below where it meets the head. Position the second pair of pliers just beneath the first, holding them in the opposite direction. Using gentle pressure, bend the fork inward.

2. Hold the bottom of the fork handle and, using the same technique as before, bend it almost entirely in toward itself. This creates a base to enable the fork to sit on the table.

3. Grasp the top of each individual fork tine and curl it under. Ensure the direction of the outer tines curl away and the inner tines curl inward.

4. Stand the fork flat and slip the place-name cards neatly in between the tines.

Betty's Top Tip

Keep your eyes peeled for old dessert and fish forks, which are often more elegant than normal dinner forks.

Bonbon dish candle

Candles create a wonderful atmosphere of romance at wedding receptions and couldn't be easier to make. Glass jars or bonbon dishes make attractive candle holders and will add a dash of vintage chic to your venue.

you will need

Glass bonbon dish

Soy wax pellets

Glass or heatproof pitcher (jug) or measuring cup

Fragrance oil

Candle wicks and wick sustainers

Wooden skewers

Ribbon

1. Measure out your wax—the amount will depend on your dish. A good rule of thumb is to fill your bonbon dish and then double the quantity. Put the wax into a pitcher (jug) and heat in a microwave on high for approximately two minutes or until it reaches melting point and is clear. Stir in a few drops of your chosen fragrance oil.

2. Cut a length of wick to reach the top of the dish, adding approximately 2 in (5 cm). Attach a sustainer to the end of the wick and place it in the center of the bonbon dish.

Betty's Top Tip

This technique works just as well with vintage china teacups, which look absolutely gorgeous in the center of your tables.

Note
Never leave lit candles unattended.

3. Carefully pour the wax in. Thread the wick between two wooden skewers resting on the rim of dish—this will hold the wick in place so that it dries straight. Let set for a few hours, then trim the wick.

4. Finish off by tying a ribbon to the stem of the dish. Make as many as required and enjoy lighting up your wedding with beautiful, decorative homemade candles.

"Something blue" garter

The garter is a centuries-old European tradition, when it was customary for the groom to throw the garter to the single men after the wedding. You can always keep yours, or make two—one to keep and one to throw! By making your own you can incorporate vintage lace to include your "something old" and by using blue ribbon, you also have your "something blue."

you will need

1¾ yd (1.6 m) lace, 6 in (15 cm) wide

Pins

1¾ yd (1.6 m) blue ribbon

Sewing machine

1¾ yd (1.6 m) elastic

Safety pin

Needle and thread

Blue-ribbon bow

1. Fold the top of the lace over by approximately ¾ in (2 cm) and pin it in place. Turn the lace over so the fold is at the back, and pin the length of blue ribbon along the lace, approximately 1¼ in (3 cm) down from the top.

2. Sew the blue ribbon in place. This will create a channel along the lace through which you can thread the elastic.

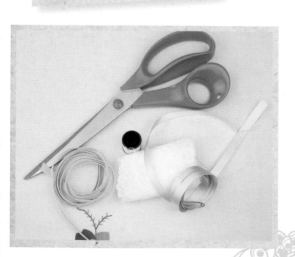

Betty's Top Tip

Rather than buying new lace you can use lace from preloved clothes or even the lace from an old tablecloth.

3. Attach a safety pin to one end of the elastic. Feed it through the lace channel until it emerges at the other end. Pull it tightly to gather the garter and create a ruffle, then tie the two pieces of elastic together.

4. Sew the two ends of lace together and attach a blue bow at the front. Your garter is ready to wear.

Shot-glass tea lights

Tea lights are an inexpensive way to add some twinkle to your wedding and this project transforms them into something pretty enough to use as a table center.

you will need

Wide lace

Shot glass

Scissors

Hot-glue gun

Narrow ribbon

Tea lights

Fabric flowers

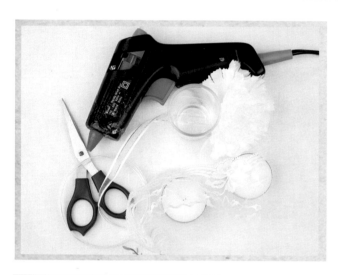

1. Measure and cut a strip of lace long enough to cover the shot glass. Stick the lace to the glass with hot glue—there is no need to put glue all over the glass, simply pull the lace around the glass and put a line of glue down one edge. This will create a neat seam.

2. Glue a length of narrow ribbon around the base of the tea light holder to make it look pretty.

Betty's Top Tip

Tea lights work equally well in decorated jars or glass candlestick holders.

3. Take a fabric flower apart until all you are left with is the bottom petals. Center the petal on the base of the tea light and glue it in place.

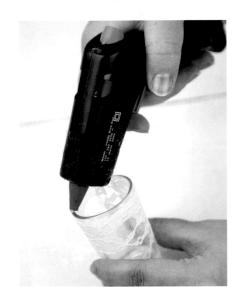

4. Apply hot glue to the rim of the shot glass and place the decorated tea light on top. Repeat to make as many tea lights as required—you can make a few and group them together or place single tea lights at the center of each table.

White felt heart decorations

Not only are these white felt hearts a lovely way to decorate your wedding reception or string between the pews at the chapel, they also subtly add fragrance throughout the day as the venue becomes warmer.

you will need

Template on page 122

Card

White felt

Sewing machine

Ribbon

Gingham or checked fabric

Dried lavender—harvested from your own garden or, if it's out of season, dried lavender can be purchased inexpensively online

Needle and thread

Fiberfill (toy) stuffing

Decorations, such as fabric flowers, beads, or charms (optional)

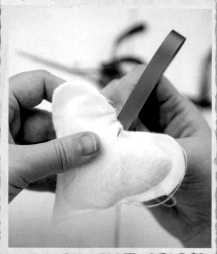

1. Copy the template on page 122 and make a card template. Use the template to cut two pieces of felt per heart decoration.

2. Either using a sewing machine or by hand, neatly sew two hearts together all the way round, leaving a gap of approximately 2 in (5 cm) in the top so you can add stuffing.

3. Push stuffing into the heart through the gap and add a little dried lavender. Continue to stuff until the heart is well shaped and firm. Before sewing the gap closed, fold a length of ribbon in half to make a loop and insert the ends into the gap. Sew the gap. Attach a ribbon bow to the join below the loop.

4. Cut a strip of gingham or checked fabric to fit across the heart. Turn under the edges all round and sew to prevent them from fraying. Sew the fabric strip in place across the front of the heart by hand with a few tiny stitches on each side. You can leave the fabric plain or add some decorations, such as a fabric flower.

Betty's Top Tip

Personalize the hearts by getting old-fashioned school name labels printed with a message. They look great sewn across the hearts and are a very inexpensive way of creating embroidered lettering.

Decorated guest flip flops in a vintage lampshade

Often by the time the evening festivities begin many ladies find their feet are suffering after so long in high heels. These decorated flip flops mean they can continue to dance the night away. By presenting them in a vintage lampshade, they won't look out of place in your beautifully decorated room.

you will need

Plain flip flops—ensure you have a variety of sizes

Hot-glue gun

Sequins and beads

An old lampshade

Tape measure

Large piece of cardboard

Scissors

Fabric roses

Tissue paper

1. Decorating your flip flops couldn't be easier. Simply pick sequins or beads that match your color scheme and, using a hot-glue gun, stick them onto the straps. Make them as glamorous as possible so your female guests will be happy to swap their high heels for your very beautiful, and comfortable, alternatives.

2. Displaying your flip flops to complement the glamour of your reception is a piece of cake. Turn the lampshade upside down so the rim is at the bottom and measure the widest part inside the shade.

3. Using the lampshade measurement, cut out a piece of cardboard to match and press this in place inside the shade, making sure that there is a gap deep enough to contain the shoes.

4. Fill the shade with tissue paper. This not only covers the cardboard but also means your flip flops will look like lovely little gifts peaking out from the paper.

Betty's Top Tip

You can replace the lampshade with an old suitcase or even fill a vintage hat box with the flip flops.

5. Decorate the edge of the shade with fabric roses. Depending on the type of fringing on your shade, these can either be tied on by their stems or glued on.

6. You could attach a little sign to the rim, inviting guests to help themselves. Now fill the lampshade with your lovely flip flops—your guests will love you for it.

Chapter 4

Crafting over Cocktails

Once you have made the decision to incorporate some homemade loveliness into your wedding, why not roll out the idea and incorporate some crafting into your bachelorette/hen celebrations? By keeping the projects really simple and the cocktails flowing, you will have a fabulous evening and maybe even make a dent in your wedding to-do list!

Paper bunting

These colorful paper flags can be hung as decorations, but also look delightful hanging on the back of chairs, or even adorning the bottom of your wedding cake. They are a great twist on fabric bunting and are very quick to make.

you will need

Template on page 122

Cardboard or card for template

Sheets of white card

Wrapping paper or découpage paper (this is ideal as it doesn't wrinkle when glued)

Scissors

Ribbon with bead embellishment, or sew beads to plain ribbon (for chair decorations, approximately ½ yd (½ m) per chair)

PVA glue

Hot-glue gun

1. Copy the template on page 122 to make a cardboard template. Use this to cut out as many white card triangles as required—you need several for making hanging bunting, or for chair decorations you need 4 or 5 per chair.

2. Use the cardboard template to cut out pairs of patterned paper triangles, to cover both sides of the bunting flags.

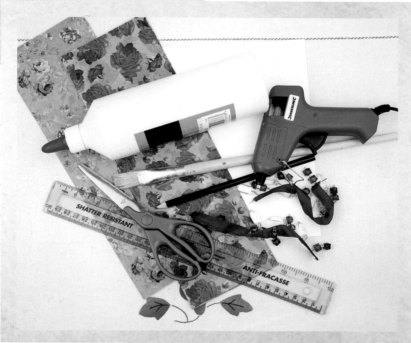

3. Brush PVA glue onto the card triangle and attach the patterned paper triangles to each side. Let dry.

4. Apply a line of hot glue along the top of the bunting triangle and stick to the length of ribbon. Attach approximately 5 flags, allowing a gap of 1 in (2.5 cm) between each one. Let dry before hanging the bejeweled bunting.

Betty's Top Tip

This idea works equally well with different paper shapes—try hearts, birds, or flowers. Think of them as a more substantial paper chain.

Jelly-bean napkin holders

If you have a sweet tooth and want a fun table decoration, this project works perfectly. The jelly beans add a wonderful pop of primary color, especially if used with crisp white napkins. If your guests get peckish, the jelly beans remain perfectly edible.

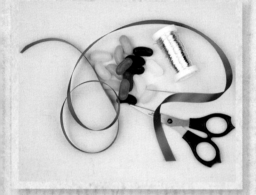

you will need

Darning needle

Jewelry wire

Scissors

Jelly beans

Ribbon

1. Thread a needle with a length of jewelry wire. Start to thread the jelly beans onto the wire, using whatever color combination you like, pushing the needle through the center of each bean.

2. Thread enough jelly beans to create a small circle, large enough to encase a napkin. Close the circle by tying both ends of the wire together and cutting.

3. To make tassels to add to the napkin ring, simply make two additional strings of jelly beans and tie them to the ring.

4. Tie a ribbon bow at the top of the tassel and they are ready to go—sweet, fun, and very inexpensive.

Betty's Top Tip

These are best made as close to your wedding day as possible, to prevent them going hard and cracking.

Confetti crackers

Throwing confetti or rice is a great wedding tradition and looks fantastic in photos. These pastel colored confetti crackers will ensure your guests have plenty to hand as you emerge as husband and wife.

you will need

White card
PVA glue
Confetti
Colored crepe paper
Ribbon
Scissors
Decorative paper flowers

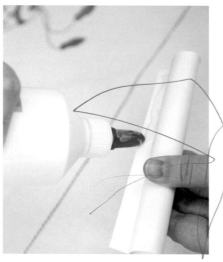

1. Cut a piece of card approximately 4 in (10 cm) square. Roll it to form a tube and then glue along the edge to secure.

2. Fill the tube with confetti, making sure that it doesn't all come out at the other end! Lay the tube flat.

Betty's Top Tip

As an alternative to crackers, fill chiffon wedding favor bags and give them to your bridesmaids and flower girls in advance. They can then hand out confetti to your guests. Always make sure your confetti is biodegradable.

3. Cut a piece of crepe paper approximately 4 x 10 in (10 x 25 cm). Wrap this around the tube, making sure the contents are safely inside, and glue the edge down to secure it. Pinch and twist each long end to resemble a cracker.

4. Stick a decorative flower in the middle of each cracker and tie a piece of ribbon around each twist. You could also attach a label, telling guests what's inside and encouraging them to pull the cracker and throw the contents!

Lollipop place-name holders

Having old-fashioned candy tables has become increasingly popular at weddings over the last few years. Guests love the nostalgia of eating licorice laces and soft chews. Why not take the idea one step further and use lollipops as place-name holders?

you will need

Crepe paper in a variety of candy shades

Scissors

Hard candy lollipops

Card

PVA glue

Self-adhesive labels

Colored or metallic pens

1. Cut a piece of crepe paper approximately 12 x 8 in (30 x 21 cm or A4 size). Place a lollipop in the center and wrap it up, twisting where the lollipop meets the stick. Tie a ribbon around the twist to secure. Trim the top of the crepe paper so that some of the lollipop stick can be seen.

2. Cut a strip of cardboard approximately 2¾ x 1¼ in (7 x 3 cm). Overlap the ends and glue them together to form a circle. This will be the stand for the lollipop, so ensure it's a snug enough fit that the lollipop doesn't fall over.

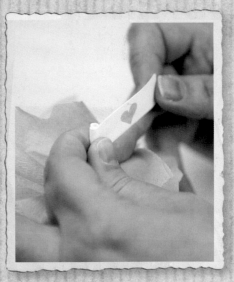

Betty's Top Tip

To make this even quicker to put together, use old-fashioned parcel labels rather than sticky labels. Instead of wrapping your lollipops, buy heart-shaped lollies and simply decorate them with ribbons and a name label.

3. Cut a small rectangle across one side of a self-adhesive label then fold it in two, leaving a small strip of sticky label exposed at one end to fix it to the lollipop stick.

4. Using colored or metallic pens, write your guest's name on the label then wrap the sticky end around the stick and place it in the stand. Repeat to make as many place names as required, using different colored paper for a "pick 'n' mix" effect. Position the lollipops at each place setting to help guests find their seat.

1920s hair comb

Hair combs are a lovely way to add subtle glamour to your wedding accessories. This comb would work perfectly for bridesmaids and flower girls. As it's such a quick and satisfying project, this is ideal for a craft inspired prewedding get-together with your friends.

you will need

Plastic hair comb

Selection of feathers—I used peacock feathers and black feathers

Felt

Scissors

Hot-glue gun

Black ribbon

Brooch

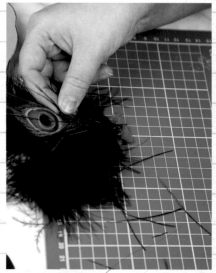

1. Arrange your feathers and when you are happy with the effect, put them to one side. Cut a small length of felt approximately 1½ x ¾ in (4 x 2 cm).

2. Use a dab of hot glue to stick your feather arrangement onto the center of the felt strip, trimming the quills if needed.

3. Cut a length of ribbon slightly longer than the felt and wrap it over the felt and the bottom of the feathers, gluing it neatly at the back.

Betty's Top Tip

You can use this technique to incorporate flowers, little birds, butterflies, even large bows into your hair accessories. You could even bake red fimo hearts in soap molds and glue those on, too.

4. Cut another piece of ribbon to match the width of the comb. Use a line of hot glue to stick the ribbon over the top of the comb, so that it covers the front and back.

5. Pin the brooch onto the center of the ribbon attached to the comb.

6. Now use a dab of hot glue to attach the feather decoration to the back of the comb, so it is displayed behind the brooch. Let dry and enjoy adding some Jazz-era chic to your big day.

Templates

All templates except the pinwheel
(See note on page 123) are at full
size and can be traced off the page.

Birdcage card holder

Page 12

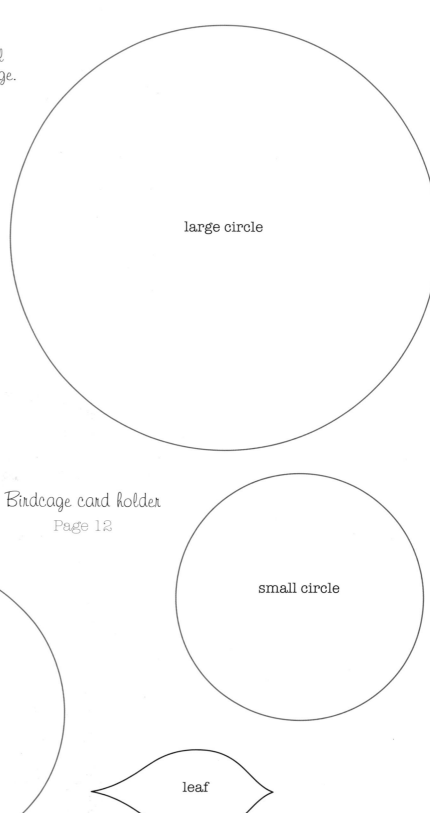

large circle

small circle

medium circle

leaf

Button bouquet
Page 50

Felt flower
table center
Page 56

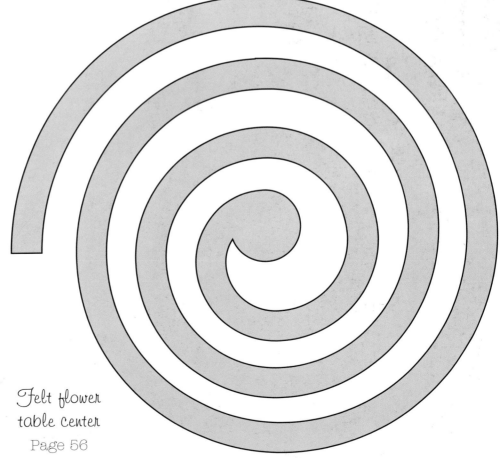

Fabric bunting
Page 82

Lips and mustache photo props
Page 62

and

Bride-and-groom brandy glasses
Page 72

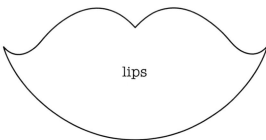

lips

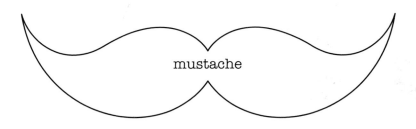

mustache

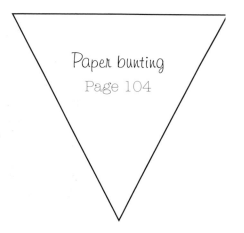

Paper bunting
Page 104

White felt heart decorations
Page 96

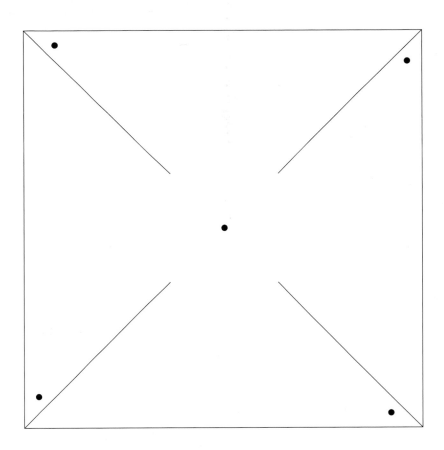

Pinwheel bouquet and buttonholes

Page 48

To make the pinwheel bouquet, photocopy the template at 200% to double its size. To make the buttonholes, use the template at this size.

Suppliers

Candle making

CandleScience (US)
http://www.candlescience.com

Full Moons Cauldron (UK)
www.fullmoons-cauldron.co.uk

Floristry

Carnmeal Cotttage (UK)
www.carnmeal.com

Floralistic (UK)
www.floralistic.co.uk

Inspirations (UK)
www.inspirationswholesale.co.uk

Jamali Floral and Garden Supplies (US)
www.jamaligarden.com

Lavenderworld (UK)
www.lavenderworld.co.uk

Lavender Green (US)
www.lavendergreen.com

Wooden Roses Factory Direct (US)
www.woodenrosesfactorydirect.com

General craft and fabric

Abakhan (UK)
www.abakhan.co.uk
For fabric, buttons, beads, jewelry wire, glue, ribbon, and trimmings.

China Presentations (UK, ships worldwide)
www.chinapresentations.net
Cake-stand fittings.

eBay
www.ebay.com and www.ebay.co.uk
For brooches, feathers, birdcages, fabric, ribbons, trims, vintage items, and much more.

Fabric Inspirations (UK)
www.fabricinspirations.co.uk
For fabric—I bought my fabric for the lampshade and bunting from here.

Hobbycraft (UK)
www.hobbycraft.co.uk

Hobby Lobby (US)
www.hobbylobby.com

Jo-Ann Fabric & Craft Stores (US)
www.joann.com

Lakeland (UK)
www.lakeland.co.uk

Michaels (US)
www.michaels.com

Replacement Pottery (UK, ships worldwide)
www.replacementpottery.co.uk
Cake-stand fittings.

SaveOnCrafts (US)
www.save-on-crafts.com
For wedding and reception supplies.

The Trimming Company (UK)
www.thetrimmingcompany.com
For sinamays, hair combs, fascinator clips.

Veilubridal (US)
www.veilubridal.com

Voirrey Embroidery Centre (UK)
Brimstage Hall Courtyard
Brimstage
Wirral
Merseyside
CH63 6JA
Tel: +44 (0) 151 342 3514
For embroidery floss (silks) and felt.

Home improvement

B & Q (UK)
www.diy.com

Lowe's Home Improvement (US)
www.lowes.com

Rightway (UK)
www.rightway.ltd.uk

Index

Acknowledgments

Thanks to my fabulous family—Mum,
Celeste, Xavier, Rowan, Nanny Rhoda, Margi,
Mark, Wan, Oliver, Grainne, Tom, and Olwyn—
and my lovely friends—Leanne, Lena, Rachel,
Sarah, and Becky T.

Picture Credits

All photography © CICO Books, except the following:

Creased paper © iStockphoto/Joan Kimball; dirty old paper—early
1900's © iStockphoto/Nicole K Cioe; horizontal ripped background paper
© iStockphoto/rami ben ami; old lined paper and old striped paper
© iStockphoto/Ursula Alter; picture frame © iStockphoto/rudi wambach;
seamless felt-textured paper © iStockphoto/rusm